Emmeline
PANKHURST

DAVID DOWNING

H www.heinemann.co.uk/library
Visit our website to find out more information about Heinemann Library books.

To order:
☎ Phone 44 (0) 1865 888066
▤ Send a fax to 44 (0) 1865 314091
💻 Visit the Heinemann Bookshop at www.heinemann.co.uk/library to browse our
catalogue and order online.

First published in Great Britain by Heinemann Library,
Halley Court, Jordan Hill, Oxford OX2 8EJ,
a division of Reed Educational and Professional Publishing Ltd.
Heinemann is a registered trademark of Reed Educational and Professional Publishing Ltd.

OXFORD MELBOURNE AUCKLAND
JOHANNESBURG BLANTYRE GABORONE
IBADAN PORTSMOUTH (NH) USA CHICAGO

Designed by AMR
Originated by Dot Gradations
Printed in China

ISBN 0 431 13869 9
06 05 04 03 02
10 9 8 7 6 5 4 3 2 1

British Library Cataloguing in Publication Data
Downing, David
 Emmeline Pankhurst. – (Leading lives)
 1.Pankhurst, Emmeline, 1858–1928 2.Suffragists – Great
 Britain – Biography – Juvenile literature 3.Great Britain –
 History – Victoria, 1837–1901 – Juvenile literature 4,Great
 Britain – History – 20th century – Juvenile literature
 I.Title
 324.6'23'092

Acknowledgements
The publishers would like to thank the following for permission to reproduce photographs:
Camera Press: p. 54; Corbis: pp. 4, 44; Hulton Archive: pp. 18, 26, 27, 30, 32, 40, 43, 47, 51; Imperial War
Museum: p. 37; Manchester Libraries: p. 6; Mary Evans: pp. 9, 10, 12, 14, 23, 29, 33, 35, 42, 46; PA Photos:
p. 52; Topham Picturepoint: pp. 16, 17, 22, 41, 48.

Cover photograph reproduced with permission of Museum of London.

Every effort has been made to contact copyright holders of any material reproduced in this book.
Any omissions will be rectified in subsequent printings if notice is given to the publishers.

Our thanks to Christopher Gibb for his comments in the preparation of this book.

Any words appearing in the text in bold, **like this**, are explained in the Glossary.

Contents

A strange welcome home

Plymouth, 4 December 1913. A ship appears on the western horizon. It is the White Star liner *Majestic*, arriving from New York. Plymouth harbour has been cleared by the authorities, and two naval gunboats are standing by to cover the approaching liner. There are police all along the docksides, and six Scotland Yard detectives are boarding a fast motor launch. They plan to intercept the *Majestic* before it docks. There are surely some extremely dangerous people on board – a gang of murderers or terrorists perhaps?

The police launch sets off, but suddenly another boat, a tug, comes into view. It is full of women, and they are trying to get to the liner first. The police launch is too fast for them. The six detectives clamber aboard, and disappear below-decks. They emerge a few minutes later with a woman in her mid-fifties. With her commanding expression, long dress, **veil** and large hat she looks like a picture of Victorian respectability, but for the last eight years she has been considered, by the government at least, as the most dangerous person in Britain.

◀ *Emmeline Pankhurst in December 1913, as she is about to leave New York and return to England, to face arrest by the British government.*

Her name is Emmeline Pankhurst, and she is the leader of the Women's Social and Political Union (WSPU), the most important of the parties fighting for **women's suffrage**, or right to vote. The women in the other boat, which proudly flies the WSPU flag, are 'suffragettes' like herself. Their campaign started out peacefully, but in recent years, under the forceful direction of Emmeline and her eldest daughter Christabel, it has grown increasingly violent. Emmeline herself has been arrested many times.

She is arrested again now, and taken aboard the police launch, much to the anger and frustration of her supporters in the tug. While Emmeline is driven across country to Exeter Prison they set fire to a huge yard full of timber at the Plymouth Docks.

Once in prison, Emmeline immediately goes on **hunger strike**, but the authorities are not concerned about that. They are determined that she will miss the welcome back meeting planned for her in London, but they have no intention of risking her death in custody. In prison or out she is a problem they cannot solve, and all they can do is keep arresting her and letting her go.

Where has this woman come from? How has she succeeded in making one of the most powerful governments in the world so terrified of her?

Statement of intent

*'Nothing has ever been got out of the British **Parliament** without something approaching a revolution.'*

(Emmeline Pankhurst)

Childhood and youth

Emmeline was born in the northern English city of Manchester on 14 July 1858. She was the first of ten children born to Robert and Jane Goulden, and would remain, throughout her childhood, the apple of her father's eye.

▲ *A residential area in Manchester in the 19th century. Emmeline grew up in a neighbourhood like this.*

The Gouldens were a prosperous family. By the time of Emmeline's birth Robert Goulden's cotton printing business was doing very well, and he had time to spare for his other favourite pursuits – amateur acting and politics. He was a prominent figure in the Manchester **Liberal Party**, and a campaigner for changes which many then considered **radical**, like the abolition of slavery in the USA. His wife Jane shared his political radicalism. She was particularly interested in gaining more rights for women.

The beginnings of a suffragette

Young Emmeline grew up in this atmosphere of enthusiasm for radical causes. Harriet Beecher Stowe's *Uncle Tom's Cabin*, the famous anti-slavery novel published in 1852, was a frequent topic of family discussion, and Emmeline was given a 'lucky bag' to collect pennies for the anti-slavery cause. She read novels from an early age. She loved stories of how the world had been turned upside-down by romantic heroes, and day-dreamed of one day making such an impact herself.

In 1867, nine-year-old Emmeline was deeply affected by an event that took place in Manchester. Three Irish rebels were hanged in public for the murder of a policeman. Though she did not see the actual hanging, Emmeline had to walk past the place of execution on her way to school each day. This troubled her, and made her think. She decided that hanging was worse than a mistake – it was a crime. She later wrote that this was when she realized 'one of the most terrible facts of life – that justice and judgement lie often a world apart'.

That same year a **bill** was passed by **Parliament** that increased the number of men who were allowed to vote in elections. An **amendment** to the bill, which gave the same rights to women, was defeated. In what was then the world's richest and most powerful country, women were still denied the right to vote. Until women had that right, as Jane Goulden patiently explained to Emmeline and her other children, there was little hope of any improvement in their situation. Women at this time were not allowed to hold official jobs or enter any profession except teaching or nursing. If a woman inherited money or property it was given to her husband when she married, and if she later left him, he kept it. He was also allowed to decide what happened to any children.

In August 1867, the Manchester **Women's Suffrage** Society was formed to campaign for women's right to vote. Five years later, the fourteen-year-old Emmeline came back from school just as her mother was setting out for one of the Society's meetings. Emmeline went with her. 'The speeches interested and excited me,' she wrote later. 'I left the meeting a conscious and confirmed suffragettist.'

Suffrage

When Emmeline was born, only around 8 per cent of men over 20 were allowed to vote. This figure was doubled and re-doubled by the Reform Acts of 1867 and 1884, but at the end of the 19th century, the vote was still restricted to less than half of the adult male population.

Paris

Soon after this, Emmeline was sent to school in the French capital Paris. There she made friends with Noémie, the daughter of the Marquis de Rochefort-Luçay. He had fought with the revolutionaries during the **Paris Commune**, and was exactly the sort of romantic hero whom Emmeline had always idolized. She quickly grew to love France, and for the rest of her life would insist that French clothes, cooking and literature were the best. She received a well-rounded education in the French school, but wondered if she would ever get to use it. At this time, girls were educated to make them more interesting companions, not to prepare them for careers.

Her school days over, Emmeline returned to the family home in Manchester. She soon grew bored. While visiting Noémie in Paris she met a young writer, who offered to marry her if her father produced a suitable **dowry**. Emmeline was not in love with the young man, but she loved the idea of leaving home and living in France. Not surprisingly, her father was less enthusiastic about the plan, and ordered her back to Manchester.

Back home, frustrated and bored, she waited for someone to rescue her from a life in which all the interesting options seemed closed, merely because she was a woman.

▲ Emmeline at the age of 17, posing in front of a painted backdrop. Her life stretched ahead of her, but her future seemed to have very little to offer.

An early lesson

'It was a custom of my father and mother to make the rounds of our bedrooms every night.... My father bent over me, shielding the candle flame with his big hand. I cannot know exactly what I thought was in his mind as he gazed down at me, but I heard him say, somewhat sadly, "What a pity she wasn't a boy"....

'I thought about my father's remarks for many days afterward.... It was made quite clear that men considered themselves superior to women, and that women accepted the situation.'

(Emmeline Pankhurst, *My Own Story*)

Marriage and London

In April 1878, Emmeline attended a **Liberal Party** rally at Manchester's Free Trade Hall. One of the speakers was Dr Richard Marsden Pankhurst, a lawyer famous for his **radical** political opinions and tireless work on behalf of the poor and disadvantaged. He had been involved in the founding of the Manchester **Women's Suffrage** Society.

After the meeting, the two were introduced. The 42-year-old Richard Pankhurst, who had always seemed too busy for marriage, was instantly captivated by the beautiful girl with the scarlet ribbons in her jet black hair. He was rather shabby and not particularly handsome, but he offered Emmeline the romantic, challenging life she wanted. Early in the following year they were married.

▲ Dr Richard Pankhurst, the famous radical captivated by Emmeline.

▲ Emmeline at the time of her wedding in 1879.

Wife and partner

As a woman of her time, Emmeline Pankhurst believed that her first duties as a wife were to look after the house and have children. In 1880 she gave birth to their first daughter Christabel, and two years later to a second, Sylvia. In 1884 the couple's first son Frank was born.

However, unlike most women of her time, Emmeline wanted to be more than just a housewife and mother, and Richard Pankhurst, unlike most men of his time, encouraged such ambition. In a love letter written before their marriage he had promised that 'every struggling cause shall be our cause', and he was true to his word. When he stood, unsuccessfully, for **Parliament** in 1883 and 1885, Emmeline was frequently by his side, helping and learning. She was still in many ways a very traditional young woman, and during the second campaign, in London's Rotherhithe, she was shocked by her husband's support for a woman candidate who wore trousers.

During this contest, Richard Pankhurst's Conservative opponent called him an atheist, someone who denies that God exists. Pankhurst sued the man for libel (making a false statement), but the judge in the case, another Conservative, told the jury to find him guilty. An enraged Emmeline wrote to the judge, accusing him of doing the **Conservative Party**'s 'dirty work' for them. She fully expected to be jailed for contempt (the crime of being disobedient to the court). She did not care – if the choice was between breaking the law and accepting injustice, she would break the law. The judge ignored her letter, but it was a clear sign of how she intended to behave in the future.

Children

After the defeat in Rotherhithe, Emmeline decided the family should move to London. Money was short, her father refused to help, and she believed her husband would find more people to appreciate him in the capital. She was pregnant with their third daughter Adela, but also had plans to open a shop selling 'nice things'. Her husband received no money for much of his political work, and she hoped that profits from the shop would help the family finances.

▲ Emmeline Pankhurst's three daughters – from left to right, Sylvia, Adela and Christabel.

The price of politics

'Waking early one Christmas morning, I examined eagerly the Christmas gifts laid out upon our beds. For Christabel there was a square box, for me an oblong box ....

'I was unable to restrain my tears when the boxes proved empty.... Though we did not know it, politics and business were putting a serious strain on our parents' financial resources; our mother had not been able to bring herself to spend money on mere Christmas presents.'

(Sylvia Pankhurst, *The Suffragette Movement*)

The Pankhurst children

	Born
Christabel	1880
Sylvia	1882
Frank	1884
Adela	1885
Harry	1889

Emerson and Company, as the shop was called, opened on the Hampstead Road in 1885. It sold fancy furniture and goods – things like Chinese teapots and Persian plates – but it never made much profit. Emmeline knew what she liked, but not what her few customers wanted, and most of the goods seemed to end up in the family home.

Such troubles faded into insignificance in September 1888. Four-year-old Frank came home one day with a cold and a cough, was wrongly diagnosed by the doctors, and died of **diphtheria** a few days later. Emmeline was terribly upset, and refused to talk of him. A year later, she almost bled to death after giving birth to another son, Harry. The maid was sent to fetch a doctor, but was refused by two on the grounds that they no longer took maternity cases. A third doctor, who obviously placed a greater value on women's lives, arrived just in time to save Emmeline's.

Russell Square

Partly to escape the memory of Frank, the family moved to a large house in Russell Square, and it was here that Emmeline Pankhurst blossomed as a hostess. The two reception rooms downstairs could be opened into one for political meetings, and she decorated them with style. She was also good at designing and making clothes that made the most of her natural beauty. One visitor to the house thought her 'a living flame, active as a bit of quicksilver, as glistening, as enticing. She was very beautiful … slender, willowy, and with exquisite features.'

▲ *A view of Russell Square, where the Pankhursts lived from 1889 to 1893.*

For a few years the Pankhurst house on Russell Square was one of London's leading political meeting places, alive with the brilliant conversation of the radical and famous. At one meeting in 1889 the Women's Franchise League (WFL) was founded to push, more strongly than the existing National Union of Women's Suffrage Societies (NUWSS), for the female vote. The refusal of the organization's treasurer, Mrs Alice Cliff, to wear a wedding ring or veil – respectably married women were supposed to wear both – was typical of the WFL's more defiant attitudes. In 1892, several WFL women even tried to break up a NUWSS meeting by force. Neither Emmeline nor Richard Pankhurst was directly involved, but both were known to favour such direct action.

During these years, women's issues were only one of the Pankhursts' interests. In the reception rooms at Russell Square

they played host to people from all across Europe –
socialists, anarchists (people who believe that no government
is necessary) and free-thinkers, who rejected all conventional
ideas – almost anyone who shared their hunger for radical, far-
reaching change. However, through it all, they remained in
many ways typical members of the privileged class – Emmeline
Pankhurst still wore a veil whenever she went out.

Political parents

Richard Pankhurst's legal practice (which paid most of the
bills), Emmeline's shop, and all the political activity left little
time for the children. However, despite the frequent absences
of their mother and father, the children grew up without any
obvious sense of resentment. They respected their father's
cleverness, loved his endearing habit of reciting poetry to
himself in the bathroom. The three daughters were all, in
different ways, inspired by his idealism, his belief that things
could get better. 'Life is nothing without enthusiasms,' he told
them. 'If you do not work for other people you will not have
been worth your upbringing.'

Emmeline Pankhurst often left the children in the care of
servants, and rarely gave them the unselfish attention they
needed. Her daughter Sylvia later wrote that she was 'rigid in
her discipline … and would tolerate no likes or dislikes'.
Sylvia's fondest memories were of herself and Christabel
joining in their parents' activities: arranging chairs, taking
collections and writing out 'To the Tea Room' signs for the
political meetings. On such occasions their mother was a
distant, almost goddess-like figure. In one edition of the *Home
News and Universal Mirror*, a family news-sheet written by the
two older daughters, one of them wrote that 'Mrs Pankhurst
looked very handsome indeed in a black sort of grenadine
[silk] with train from the shoulders'.

Coming into her own

In the winter of 1892–93, the 100-year lease (rental agreement) ran out on the Russell Square house, and Richard Pankhurst received a large and unexpected bill for 100 years' worth of wear and tear. Financial strain and incessant travelling – most of his legal work remained in the north – affected his health, and with Emmeline Pankhurst's shop making no money, there was little reason to keep the family in London. After seven years in the capital they moved back to Manchester, eventually settling into a large suburban house in the Victoria Park area.

Christabel and Sylvia, now fourteen and twelve years old, were sent to Manchester High School for Girls. In London they had never gone to school. Their mother had worried that an official education would fill their heads with love of the British Empire and other backward-looking nonsense, and deprive them of their precious originality.

◀ *Emmeline Pankhurst in early middle age. Despite being a* **radical**, *she always liked to look like a pillar of respectability.*

From Liberal to Labour

Emmeline Pankhurst, while remaining a leading member of the London-based Women's Franchise League, quickly re-established her links with the Manchester **Women's Suffrage** Society, and late in 1893 was voted onto its executive committee, the group which made the decisions. The following year she helped to organize a large demonstration in Manchester's Free Trade Hall.

The pressure for change was beginning to have its effect. In 1893, New Zealand had become the first country to give women the vote, and in 1894 the British **Parliament** passed a new Local Government Act which gave married women the right to stand for local office. Emmeline immediately got herself elected onto her local Board of **Poor Law** Guardians, the institution that was supposed to provide help for the neediest members of the community.

▶ *A child worker in a cotton mill in the late 19th century. Emmeline Pankhurst considered it her duty to improve the lot of such disadvantaged members of society.*

Such changes were, of course, welcome, but far too slow in coming for the Pankhursts. They had never expected anything from the **Conservative Party**, and by this time they had almost given up on the **Liberal Party** as well. More and more, they placed their hopes in the new **socialist** movements, which believed in putting the interests of ordinary working people above those of the traditional ruling classes. In 1892, Keir Hardie, a man the Pankhursts both liked and respected, had become the first socialist Member of Parliament (MP), and when he formed the **Independent Labour Party (ILP)** in 1893 they were among the first to join.

▲ *Keir Hardy, who founded the Independent Labour Party.*

This decision was not appreciated by many of Richard Pankhurst's legal clients, and they withdrew their business. The family struggled on financially, and the new house in Victoria Park became as busy a political meeting place as the old one in Russell Square. In 1895 Richard Pankhurst stood as an ILP candidate in the general election. Emmeline helped with his campaign, and on one occasion was subjected to a hail of stones from some Conservative hooligans. Her husband was still much too **radical** for most people's tastes, and lost once again.

Boggart Hole Clough

Emmeline, meanwhile, was coming into her own as a Poor Law Guardian. After a sharp rise in unemployment had increased the numbers of those in need, she helped to organize soup kitchens, where poor people were given free meals, and then bullied the local authorities into creating much-needed projects to provide employment. Her combination of lady-like respectability and passionate radicalism proved irresistible, and her popularity among local people soared.

As the now-undisputed leader of the Board she set out to reform the whole system, and soon the staffs of the various workhouses (the government-run houses where poor people could live and work) came to dread the prospect of a visit from the terrifying Mrs Pankhurst. Corrupt and incompetent staff were shown the door, and the conditions for many inmates improved dramatically. Meals were made more nutritious, children given warm clothing, the old provided with comfortable chairs. She even managed to persuade her fellow Guardians to build cottages in the country for the care of orphans.

In 1896 her fame spread still further. Manchester City Council decided to ban political gatherings in public parks, including one – Boggart Hole Clough – which the ILP regularly used for its meetings. The ILP ignored the ban, and two of its speakers were arrested, fined, and then jailed when they refused to pay. Emmeline was the next to speak, and she too was arrested. In court she conducted her own defence, and told the judge she would go to jail rather than pay a fine.

The judge did not dare to jail such a respectable, and well-known, woman. Five times he asked her to change her mind, but every Sunday she turned up at Boggart Hole Clough to repeat her offence in front of ever-larger crowds.

The press, torn between respect for the law and admiration for Emmeline's defiance, eventually came out on her side, and the prosecution was dropped.

A terrible shock

By 1898 Richard Pankhurst's health, worn down by financial worries and overwork, had worsened. That summer he managed to find the money for Emmeline and eighteen-year-old Christabel to visit Noémie in France, but his condition suddenly deteriorated while they were away. Sixteen-year-old Sylvia, who had been left behind to look after him, could only watch in despair as the doctors failed to save him.

Emmeline hurried back from France in vain. Arriving at Manchester Station she saw the news 'Dr Pankhurst Dead' emblazoned across the newspaper placards. Her husband and political partner was gone.

Visiting the workhouse

'The first time I went into the place I was horrified to see little girls seven and eight years of age on their knees scrubbing the cold stones of the long corridors. These little girls were clad, summer and winter, in thin cotton frocks, low in the neck and short-sleeved ....

'I also found pregnant women in the workhouse, scrubbing floors, doing the hardest kind of work, almost until their babies came into the world. Many of them were unmarried women, very, very young, mere girls. These poor mothers were allowed to stay in the hospital after confinement [giving birth] for a short two weeks. Then they had to make a choice of staying in the workhouse and earning their living by scrubbing and other work, in which case they were separated from their babies ...or they could leave – leave with a two-week-old baby in their arms without hope, without home, without money, without anywhere to go.'

(Emmeline Pankhurst, My Own Story)

The WSPU

Richard Pankhurst left no money, only debts. Emmeline, who had just turned 40 years old, moved the family into a smaller house, optimistically opened another shop, and found herself a paying job as a local government **Registrar of Births and Deaths**. This position gave her further opportunities to observe how badly women were treated, and how badly they needed the vote.

A political family

There was no cooling of political passion after the death of her husband. The **Second Boer War** broke out in the British colonies in southern Africa in 1899; Emmeline Pankhurst, like the more **radical socialists**, spoke out against it. This was not a popular position, as most of the family soon discovered. Eleven-year-old Harry was knocked unconscious by a fellow pupil for opposing the war, and his sister Adela had her cheek badly cut by a thrown book. Sylvia, now at Manchester Art School, was almost expelled for expressing her anti-war opinions, and several windows of the new family home were broken by stone-throwers. Richard Pankhurst would have been proud of his family.

After her father's death Christabel had stayed on in France, and when she returned it was to work, rather grudgingly, in the family shop. She was rescued from this job by a couple of new friends, who encouraged her to join them in spreading the **women's suffrage** message among the working women of the area. Rather to her own surprise, Christabel found she was good at public speaking, and her new political enthusiasm was catching. By 1902 she had persuaded both her mother and her sister Sylvia to join her in mounting a major new campaign for women's suffrage.

▲ *Emmeline sitting at her desk in the early years of the struggle. Many women wrote to her for encouragement and inspiration.*

The ILP and the WSPU

Emmeline Pankhurst was now on the **ILP**'s leadership committee, and like Sylvia she assumed that any suffrage campaign would be carried out in partnership with the ILP. Christabel was not convinced that this was a good idea: she suspected the male-dominated ILP would, in the long run, prove as unhelpful as the other political parties. Her suspicions were confirmed when women were barred from a new party meeting hall in Manchester. This hall was named after Richard Pankhurst, which made his wife and daughters even more angry.

A week later they and other ILP women formed a new organization, the Women's Social and Political Union (WSPU), at the Pankhurst home. This was intended by many as a sort of semi-independent group set up within the party to argue for women's suffrage. However, even those women most committed to the ILP found it hard to put up with some of the men's comments: the future Labour Prime Minister Ramsay MacDonald, for example, dismissed the WSPU as 'tomfoolery'. Other women, like Christabel, were quite prepared for a break in the not-too-distant future.

▲ A council of war at the Clement's Inn headquarters of the Women's Social and Political Union. Christabel Pankhurst is second from the left, Emmeline second on the right.

Last chance

Emmeline, though pessimistic, was reluctant to give up all hope of peacefully persuading **Parliament** to give women the vote. There was no possibility of an ILP government in the near future – the party still had only a handful of MPs – and little chance that the **Liberals** could be shamed into introducing a government **bill**. However, perhaps the House as a whole could be persuaded by public pressure into passing a **private member's bill**. In early 1905, Emmeline convinced the Liberal MP Bamford Slack to sponsor such a bill, and then spent almost three months in London trying to persuade his fellow MPs to support it.

How laws are changed

In Great Britain, both then and now, possible new laws are presented to the Houses of Parliament in the form of bills which list the details of the proposed changes. Most are government bills (the government having been formed by the party that has won the most seats in Parliament through elections), but time is also made for a very limited number of private member's bills, which are presented by individual Members of Parliament of all parties. Bills are debated and then usually voted on. In some cases MPs have 'talked out' bills, continuing with the debate until the time allowed for a vote has been used up. Those bills that are voted on, and win majority support, become laws.

Her efforts were in vain. On 12 May 1905 Slack's bill was talked out (see box) by two determined opponents of women's rights. Emmeline and other campaigners mounted a peaceful protest outside the House, but only the police seemed interested. How could they make people listen?

The only conclusion

Back in Manchester Emmeline, Christabel and Sylvia went over the arguments. Neither the **Conservatives** nor the Liberals seemed likely to offer women the vote, and the ILP, if it ever came to power, might well prove just as bad as the older parties. As had just been demonstrated, a private member's bill had little or no chance of success.

The conclusion was obvious. If women could not expect anything from the political parties, they would have to win the vote by their own efforts. Because there were no women in Parliament, the battle would have to be fought outside, in the public halls and on the streets.

'We women are roused'

Emmeline Pankhurst and her two older daughters were all passionately committed to the struggle, but, fortunately for the Women's Social and Political Union (WSPU), each attracted a different group of supporters. Emmeline and Christabel, respectable in appearance and very conventional in their non-political beliefs, appealed to **middle-class** women of their own generations who had suffered or expected to suffer from the limitations placed on women in a male-dominated society. The unconventional and artistic Sylvia appealed to those in search of a deeper, more emotional rebellion against society as a whole. For Sylvia, the oppression of women was not only wrong in itself, it offered clear evidence that something more basic was wrong with the way people treated each other.

The Pankhurst spectre

Inspired by this trio of remarkable women, new recruits rushed to join the WSPU. Annie Kenney, a young mill worker from an educated family, was one, and it was she who joined Christabel in the famous demonstration that ignited the next phase of the struggle. The **Liberal Party** seemed certain to win the general election in January 1906, so the WSPU decided to pressurize Liberal candidates on their attitude towards **women's suffrage**. On 13 October 1905, two Liberal leaders – Winston Churchill and Lord Grey – were the main speakers at a Liberal Rally in Manchester. Both men were said to be supporters of women's suffrage, but when Christabel and Annie shouted the question 'Will the Liberal Government give votes to women?' they were ignored. When they unfurled a 'Votes for Women' banner they were dragged from their seats by stewards and policemen, taken outside and arrested. The next morning they refused to pay a fine and were sent to prison for a week.

▲ *Suffragettes drawing on the pavement, March 1913. This was one of many tactics they devised to spread their message.*

Emmeline, who had offered to pay the fines but was overruled by Christabel, led a series of 'indignation meetings' and organized a triumphal party to celebrate the pair's release. The newspapers spread the story around the country, inspiring more women to join the WSPU. Soon Liberal meetings up and down the country were being interrupted by angry women. At one such meeting in Cheshire, the future Prime Minister Lloyd George spoke of 'the Pankhurst spectre' – a haunting sign of trouble to come. The Liberals won the election with ease, but this spectre would haunt them for years.

'Suffragettes'

Emmeline Pankhurst had canvassed for **ILP** leader Keir Hardie in the election, and Hardie repaid her by bringing two important recruits to the WSPU. Frederick and Emmeline Pethick-Lawrence were wealthy **socialists** and good organizers with many influential friends, and for the next six years their flat in Clement's Inn, London, served as the WSPU's headquarters.

FOR MORE ON THE KEY PEOPLE IN EMMELINE PANKHURST'S TIME, SEE PAGES 59–60.

In July 1906, Christabel moved from Manchester to Clement's Inn to become the WSPU's Chief Organizer. She decided to mount more demonstrations in the hope that the government would over-react. She knew that a war fought to safeguard male privileges could only, in the long run, make the government look bad, not to mention ridiculous.

▶ *Teresa Billington carrying a suffragette banner outside the Houses of Parliament.*

There was heckling (interrupting speakers) in the House of Commons, groups of representatives were sent to **Downing Street**, and there was personal harassment of government ministers. The *Daily Mail* started to call the protesters 'suffragettes', a term first used in the USA as early as 1869. That summer Annie Kenney, Teresa Billington and two others attacked the country house of Prime Minister Asquith, and became the first suffragettes to be sent to Holloway Prison.

For pity's sake

'Put me on an island where the girls are few
Put me among the most ferocious lions in the zoo
You can put me on a treadmill and I'll never, never fret
But for pity's sake don't put me near a suffragette'

(A popular song of the time. Its open mockery of the suffragettes concealed a considerable degree of male fear and anxiety. Equality between men and women seemed a frightening idea to many in the first decade of the 20th century.)

Roving ambassador

Through 1906 Emmeline Pankhurst held on to her job as a **Registrar of Births and Deaths**. The family's finances were as precarious as ever, but by early 1907 it was clear she had to choose between doing her job properly and playing a leading role in the WSPU. In March 1907 she gave up her job, and for the next seven years, while Christabel directed operations from the centre, her mother would be the WSPU's roving ambassador and chief spokesperson. She would have no real home, staying in hotel rooms and the homes of her many supporters.

Emmeline found new friends and supporters wherever she went, but she also found enemies. Like other WSPU speakers, she had stones, eggs and rotten vegetables thrown at her. Men shouted out dirty jokes, sang insulting songs and tried to drown out her voice by shouting and stamping their feet. In a Devon by-election campaign (to elect an MP outside a normal general election) early in 1908, angry opponents were about to stuff Pankhurst into a barrel and roll her down a hill when police intervened. The blows to the head and wrenched ankle she received during this tussle left her in pain for months.

Pin-ups

Not all of the Pankhursts' arguments were with their opponents. By the end of 1907 some members of the WSPU were tired of taking orders from Christabel and Emmeline. The movement, these women argued, should become more **democratic**, with annual conferences and clear records of what the money was being spent on. Several members left to form the Women's Freedom League, but most were quite happy to accept the Pankhursts' orders. By this time Christabel was regarded as a political genius, and Emmeline as a fighting saint, a modern Joan of Arc. Many WSPU members wore brooches containing pictures of the two women, and their portraits, like those of future pop stars, decorated thousands of bedroom walls.

▶ *Christabel and Emmeline Pankhurst in 1908.*

▲ *Suffragettes marching to Hyde Park on 21 June 1908.*

In February 1908, Emmeline Pankhurst led an attempt to break through a police cordon around the House of Commons, and received her first prison term. During the six-week sentence she made a public appeal for women to raise funds for the WSPU by observing a week of self-denial, putting the needs of the cause of women's suffrage before their own needs. The response was tremendous. Women deprived themselves of meals and walked to work to save money; some even busked on the street, performing in public for donations. Immediately after her release, Pankhurst took part in a rally at London's Albert Hall. The audience roared with joy, stretched out their arms in adoration, and piled their wedding rings on the collection plates being handed round. 'The old cry was, "You will never rouse women",' Pankhurst told them. 'But we have done what they thought – and hoped – to be impossible. We women are roused.'

A dictator

*'She was ruthless in using the followers she gathered around her, as she was ruthless to herself ... She was a most astute statesman, a skilled politician, a self-dedicated reshaper of the world – and a **dictator** without mercy.'*

(Emmeline Pankhurst as described by Teresa Billington, who left the WSPU in protest against the organization's lack of democracy)

Fighting the good fight

Through the summer of 1908 the campaign rumbled on. Both Emmeline and Christabel spoke in London's Hyde Park at a June rally which drew half a million spectators. Four months later both were on the platform in Trafalgar Square when Christabel urged their followers to 'rush' **Parliament** when it met in three days' time. The two Pankhursts were arrested on a charge of 'inciting to violence', and three days later an army of 5000 policemen struggled to control the suffragette army in Parliament Square.

Trial and prison

At their trial Christabel cross-examined **Chancellor of the Exchequer** Lloyd George and **Home Secretary** Herbert Gladstone, both of whom had been subpoenaed (ordered) to appear at her insistence. Was it not true that women were only using the same kind of tactics that men had once used to attain the same rights, she asked? They had to admit that it was.

A studio recording

'The reasons why women should have the vote should be obvious to every fair-minded person. Taxation and representation should go together, therefore women taxpayers are entitled to the vote. Men got the vote not by persuading but by alarming the legislators. Similar methods must be adopted by women. The militant methods of women today are clearly thought out and vigorously pursued. We have waited too long for political justice. We refuse to wait any longer.'

(A political message recorded by Christabel Pankhurst in early 1909, and distributed as a recording disc)

Both Emmeline and Christabel were sentenced to ten weeks in Holloway Prison. Emmeline refused to be stripped and searched, to undress in public, or to obey the rule of silence. In fact, she deliberately broke the last rule, chatting with Christabel in the exercise yard. The authorities threw her into solitary confinement (isolated her in a separate cell), which affected both her nerves and her physical health. Only the distant sound of the Women's Social and Political Union (WSPU) bands, singing as they circled the jail, kept her spirits up.

▲ Emmeline and Christabel Pankhurst in their Holloway Prison clothes, late 1908.

A well-advertised welcoming-out party greeted the two women on their release. The WSPU rarely missed an opportunity to publicize their cause, and great care was always taken to make such occasions as eye-catching as possible. Sylvia Pankhurst, with her artistic eye and training, helped stage many of these occasions, and also designed many of the WSPU brooches, posters and banners.

Hitting harder

During Emmeline and Christabel's imprisonment the suffragette campaign had grown bolder. In those days politicians were not surrounded by security people, and women accosted and harassed government ministers outside their houses and churches, on railway stations, even on golf courses. In 1907, uninvited women had been banned from attending ministers' public meetings, but WSPU members gained entrance in a number of ingenious ways, from disguising themselves as men to lowering themselves through roof windows on ropes.

▼ *The Editorial Department of the Women's Social and Political Union at Lincoln's Inn House. Most of the women who worked there were volunteers.*

Several women chained themselves to iron railings in **Downing Street** or Parliament Square. Bands of WSPU women leapt from furniture vans, confused the police by knocking off their helmets, and immobilized their horses by striking the joints of their rear legs, which forced them to sit down. Other groups of women toured the streets in fake prison vans, which bore the initials EP (for Emmeline Pankhurst) rather than the official ER (for the king, Edward Rex).

In October 1908 the first deliberate damage to property occurred when stones were used to break several Downing Street windows. Early in the following year a woman in Bristol hit government minister Winston Churchill with a horse-whip, shouting, 'take that in the name of the insulted women of England'. More and more women were sent to prison, and early in 1909 one of them, the sculptress Marion Wallace Dunlop, became the first to go on **hunger strike**. Others soon followed, and in June, following a major battle and over 100 arrests in Parliament Square, the prison authorities resorted to **force-feeding** for the first time. In Parliament a raging Keir Hardie called it a 'horrible bestial outrage', but other MPs just laughed and cheered.

Force feeding

'Six hefty wardresses [female prison officers] would fling her on her back and hold her down by the shoulders, wrists, hips, knees and ankles. Then the doctor forced open the lips, inserted a steel probe through a gap in the clenched teeth, screwed open her mouth, and thrust the tube down her throat. Her scraped gums bled profusely and the feeding tube was often coughed up and had to be reinserted. This operation was repeated two, sometimes three, times a day.'

(A description of force-feeding taken from David Mitchell's *The Fighting Pankhursts*)

TREATMENT OF POLITICAL PRISONERS UNDER A LIBERAL GOVERNMENT

▲ *A suffragette poster, advising voters that they can only stop the force-feeding of women by voting against their government.*

Triumph and tragedy

Not surprisingly, such contempt merely swelled the ranks of the suffragettes. By the end of 1909 enthusiasm for the movement was greater than ever: the WSPU's income had risen from £3000 in 1906–7 to £32,000 in 1909–10, and over 100 women were now employed on a full-time basis. The press was mostly supportive. The suffragettes had won all the arguments except the one that mattered most, the one with the government. A general election was called for January 1910. The Liberal leader Asquith hinted that he would bring in a **women's suffrage bill**, and Christabel decided to give him the benefit of the doubt. She called a temporary halt to hostilities.

In the meantime, Pankhurst's son Harry, now 21 years old, was taken ill with poliomyelitis, which affects the central nervous system. Rather than stay with him, Pankhurst went off on a pre-arranged speaking tour of the USA. She probably hoped to bring back the money needed for Harry's treatment, but he died soon after her return in January 1910.

A grief-stricken Pankhurst told friends to behave 'as if no great sorrow had come just now. It breaks me down to talk about it although I am very grateful for sympathy. I want to get through my work and know that you will help me do it.'

'Black Friday'

The 1910 election result was a triumph for the WSPU – their campaigning cost the Liberals 40 seats. An all-party group in the House of Commons was formed to come up with a women's suffrage bill, but it was still under consideration when Asquith ordered a dissolution of Parliament for completely separate reasons, and the bill failed to become law.

The suffragettes were outraged, and on 19 November – or 'Black Friday' as it came to be called – Pankhurst led a group of over 300 women to confront Parliament. There was a five-hour battle, which included hand-to-hand fighting and a lot of window-breaking. Three days later Pankhurst led an attack on Downing Street. Prime Minister Asquith, surrounded by angry women, had to be rescued and driven away in a taxi.

The Liberals won another election, but the women's suffrage bill was not revived. Asquith merely offered to add an **amendment** promising women's suffrage to a bill extending male suffrage.

Pankhurst was on a speaking tour of the USA and Canada at the time this was announced. She called Asquith's offer 'an insult to women' and announced that she was 'ready to renew the fight'.

▲ *Emmeline, Christabel and Sylvia Pankhurst at Waterloo Station in October 1911. By this time Sylvia's views had become very different from those of her mother and elder sister.*

The suffragette war

Until 1912 the suffragette protests had stopped short of deliberate attempts to injure people or cause serious property damage, but Asquith's failure to deliver a **women's suffrage bill** forced Emmeline and Christabel to think again. They remained unwilling to risk life, but decided to intensify attacks against property. 'If it is necessary,' Christabel said, 'we shall not hesitate to burn a palace. We shall terrorize the lot of you.'

'Torturing innocent women'

Emmeline kicked off the new policy in March. She broke several windows of the Prime Minister's house at 10 **Downing Street**. She was arrested, but over the next few days London echoed to the sound of breaking glass. The government tried to arrest all the other Women's Social and Political Union (WSPU) leaders, but Christabel managed to escape to Paris. For the next two and a half years she would direct the suffragette campaign from the French capital. Her mother and the Pethick-Lawrences, who had been sentenced to nine months in prison, immediately went on **hunger strike**. When the doctors and female prison officers arrived to **force-feed** her, Pankhurst threatened them with a wash-jug. Realizing that she would only submit to force, and afraid that they might kill her, the authorities released her the next day.

Most of her supporters were not so lucky. Younger suffragettes like Sylvia Pankhurst were force-fed many times, and even the Pethick-Lawrences were made to endure it. This intensely painful process appalled many people. 'You will go down in history as the man who tortured innocent women,' the famous **socialist** MP George Lansbury told Prime Minister Asquith in the House of Commons.

Property damage

Christabel launched a campaign of **arson**. Suffragette volunteers were given petrol, fuses, tools and an empty house. The first attempts, in the summer of 1912, were a failure, but a campaign against the Royal Mail, which involved either setting fire to postboxes or filling them with sticky substances, destroyed tens of thousands of letters. There was more window smashing and an epidemic of false fire alarms. More amusingly, small WSPU banners were substituted for all the flags on the King's golf course at Balmoral in Scotland.

Life and property

'There is something that governments care more for than human life, and that is the security of property. So it is through property that we shall strike the enemy.'

(Emmeline Pankhurst at the Albert Hall, October 1912)

This new campaign was not to everyone's taste. Both Sylvia and the Pethick-Lawrences disliked it, and the latter insisted that it could only continue if Christabel returned from France to direct it in person. Christabel refused, saying that the movement needed a leader with a cool head to remain free. The Pethick-Lawrences resigned from the WSPU. At an Albert Hall rally in October 1912 Pankhurst paid tribute to their contribution over the years, but in private she was less generous. She never spoke to the Pethick-Lawrences again.

Through 1913 the attacks on property grew more violent. Street lamps were broken, railway seats slashed, public flowerbeds destroyed. Slogans were burnt across golf and bowling greens with acid, telephone wires were cut. Several large houses were burnt down, and a group led by Emily Wilding Davison managed to blow up Lloyd George's new house at Walton Heath.

▲ *St Catherine's Church in Hatcham, South London, one of the buildings burnt down by the suffragettes.*

When Pankhurst announced this bombing to the world she was arrested again and sentenced to three years in prison. Once again she went on hunger strike, but this time the prison authorities let her condition weaken before they released her.

Turning Britain upside-down

'Our task was to show the Government that it was expedient
[in its own interest] to yield to the women's just demands. In
order to do that we had to make England and every department
of English life insecure and unsafe. We had to make English law a
failure and the courts farce comedy theatres; we had to discredit
the Government and **Parliament** in the eyes of the world; we had
to spoil English sports, hurt business, destroy valuable property,
demoralise the world of [the upper class of] society, shame the
churches, upset the whole orderly conduct of life.'

(Emmeline Pankhurst, writing in *My Own Story* about the
situation in early 1913)

The government had introduced
a new law that allowed them to
release hunger-strikers, and then
re-arrest them once they had
recovered their strength. This
law soon became known as the
'Cat and Mouse Act', because it
seemed as if the government
was playing with the suffragettes
the way a cat plays with a
mouse. Over the next year
Emmeline was re-arrested ten
times, and most of the other
leaders were treated similarly.

▶ *The Cat and Mouse Act, as
pictured in a famous WSPU poster.*

However, the government could not defeat the suffragettes. In June 1913, in the most dramatic of all suffragette protests, Emily Wilding Davison seized hold of the King's horse during the Derby horse race at Epsom, and was battered to death by its hooves. Thousands of women followed her funeral procession through the streets of London.

▲ The funeral of Emily Wilding Davison, who threw herself in front of the King's horse at the Derby.

Appealing to the King

Pankhurst spent the summer of 1913 working on her autobiography, *My Own Story*, in Paris. In October she travelled to the USA for a series of speaking engagements, but was detained at the Ellis Island immigration centre in New York Bay as an 'undesirable alien'. After threatening a hunger strike, the American President Wilson intervened to get her released, and a few weeks later she returned to the UK with £4500 – a very large sum in those days – for the WSPU.

She was immediately arrested and taken to Holloway Prison, where she began yet another hunger strike. A few days later the King was happily watching the opera *Joan of Arc* from his royal box when two suffragettes started shouting at him through a megaphone from the box opposite: 'Do you realize that women today are fighting, as Joan of Arc fought, for human liberty, and are also being tortured and done to death in the name of the King by a despicable government? Are you aware that Mrs Pankhurst is at this moment suffering agony in prison on your authority?'

▶ *Emmeline Pankhurst being arrested outside Buckingham Palace, 1914.*

A family split

There was also trouble in the Pankhurst family. Over the years the WSPU had drifted further and further away from socialism, and in 1912 Christabel had virtually declared war on their socialist allies. This had appalled both Sylvia and Adela, who remained true to their father's vision of a socialism that included complete equality for women. Emmeline persuaded Adela to help the women's movement in Australia, but Sylvia was not so easy to deal with. She had built up an army of passionate supporters among working people in East London, and refused to accept Christabel's leadership. Christabel would not tolerate this. In February 1914, Sylvia's East London branch of the WSPU was expelled from the organization. Relationships between Sylvia, Emmeline and Christabel would never be the same again.

▲ Sylvia Pankhurst speaking to a crowd in London's East End. Unlike Emmeline and Christabel, she opposed World War I and supported the **communist** revolution in Russia.

World War I

The last act of the suffragette drama was unfolding. In the first seven months of 1914, railway stations, churches, a racecourse grandstand and three Scottish castles were destroyed by suffragette action. In London, the Albert Hall's organ was flooded, and a famous painting in the National Gallery – Velazquez's *Venus Before Her Mirror* – was slashed by a suffragette named Mary Richardson, who said she was protesting against the persecution of Emmeline Pankhurst, 'the most beautiful personality of the age'. Christabel was sure that victory was near, that a government facing war in Ireland, increasing trade union hostility and a general election could no longer afford its war on women. She was probably right, but all calculations were suddenly thrown into doubt by the outbreak of World War I.

Women and war

On 13 August 1914, nine days after Britain had declared war on Germany, the WSPU announced that their campaign had ended. In September Emmeline and Christabel Pankhurst publicly announced their support for the war. They took an even more **patriotic** line than most men, demanding that all men should join the armed forces and that all women should work in industry.

Why they did so is hard to say. Christabel said a German victory would be disastrous for women, but there is little evidence that German women were treated much worse than British women at this time. Perhaps Emmeline and Christabel were simply caught up in the general surge of patriotism. In 1915 they organized a 'Women's Right to Serve' demonstration, and Emmeline stood on a platform alongside her old enemies Lloyd George and Winston Churchill as a long procession of women war-workers marched past.

FOR MORE ON THE KEY PEOPLE OF EMMELINE PANKHURST'S TIME, SEE PAGES 59–60.

▲ Women demanding the right to work during World War I,
17 July 1915.

Both Adela and Sylvia opposed the war, deepening the rift with
their mother. Sylvia also attacked her mother for not insisting
on equal pay for all the women working in the war industries.
Emmeline criticized such 'foolish and unpatriotic conduct' and
publicly regretted that she could not stop her two younger
daughters from using the family name.

Triumph and anti-climax

On a long tour of America in 1918 Pankhurst demanded military
intervention to end the **communist** regime in Russia, and told
her audiences the communists had 'declared all women over
eighteen to be national property, subject to a system of free love'.
Back in England she toured the factories as part of a government
campaign to combat communism among the workers.

The socialism of her younger years had been thrown aside, but her deepest political desire was about to be granted. The suffragettes had been on the verge of victory in 1914 and now they were pushing at an already opening door. In all parts of the economy women had shown they were the equal of men, and the 'responsible' attitude of leaders like Pankhurst during the war was widely admired. By 1918 there were few prepared to deny them the vote, and in June a **Women's Suffrage Bill** finally passed through **Parliament**. Only women aged over 30 were given the vote, but it was generally accepted that it was merely a matter of time before men and women voted on an equal basis. The battle had been won.

▲ *A young woman working in an arms factory during World War I.*

▲ *Christabel Pankhurst campaigning in London, October 1917.*

In September 1918 a new law allowed women to stand for election to Parliament. The WSPU was renamed the Women's Party, and it was announced that Christabel would contest a seat in the Birmingham suburb of Smethwick in that December's general election. The Women's Party opposed the socialism that Sylvia favoured; they called for trade unions to be abolished and for government control of wages and working conditions. The government Emmeline and Christabel wanted would be well-meaning and generous, but would tolerate no challenge to its authority. Britain would be expected to obey orders, rather like the old WSPU.

Emmeline and Christabel campaigned hard, but their extreme patriotism was no longer fashionable and people resented their certainty that they knew best. Christabel lost the election, giving Emmeline what she called 'the bitterest disappointment of her life'. Suddenly their future looked bleak.

Crusader without a crusade

Now that the vote had been won (at least for those aged over 30), politically active women turned their attention to other issues that deeply affected female lives. Organizations like the National Union of Women's Suffrage Societies and the Women's Freedom League began campaigning for such things as earlier sex education, greater access to methods of birth control, and equal educational opportunities for boys and girls. Emmeline and Christabel Pankhurst, who had done so much to make such questioning possible, were not comfortable with these moves towards women's social and sexual independence. At heart they were children of the Victorian age, out of place in the world after World War I, and the Women's Party soon collapsed from lack of support.

North America

They had no money, but they did have fame. In September 1919 Emmeline set sail for New York to start another lecture tour. The USA was in the middle of a 'red scare' (a time of exaggerated fear of **communism**), and her anti-communist message was very popular. She was paid $500 a lecture, a small fortune in those days.

In Britain her popularity was waning. There was a poor response to an event to raise funds for her and Christabel. Only £3000 of the £10,000 target was raised. Half of it was spent on a cottage in Devon, but only Christabel used it. Emmeline stayed in North America, moving north to Canada at the end of 1919, and continuing her anti-communist lecture tour. In 1920 the Canadian National Council for Combating Venereal Diseases, which had films, literature and clinics ready for a major campaign against the diseases transmitted by sexual intercourse, hired Emmeline as their star speaker.

Christabel joined her in the summer of 1922, and the two set up home together in Toronto, but Emmeline continued to spend most of her time touring. Her health suffered from the constant travelling, but sitting at home doing nothing left her feeling bored and restless. It was only when she suddenly collapsed in the autumn of 1924 that she could be persuaded to take a long rest on the island of Bermuda. Once recovered, her restlessness soon resurfaced, and in the summer of 1925 she and Christabel opened The English Tea Shop of Good Hope in Juan les Pins on the French Riviera. Like Emerson and Company 40 years earlier, it was a flop.

Home again

At the end of 1925 Pankhurst returned to Britain for the first time in six years. She refused the leadership of a campaign to win the vote for women aged under 30, preferring to concentrate on her dislike of communism, which she now defined widely enough to include most **socialists**. During the **General Strike** of 1926 she offered her help to the government, and early the following year agreed to stand as a **Conservative** candidate in London's East End, the area where her **estranged** daughter Sylvia had been so popular.

Sylvia was still active in many socialist and women's campaigns, and in 1927 she caused a sensation by announcing that she was having a child outside marriage and refusing to name the father.

Emmeline had not spoken to Sylvia since the beginning of World War I, and when she found out about the baby, in the spring of 1928, she wept uncontrollably. She would have to abandon politics, she said, because she was too ashamed ever to appear in public again.

In May 1928, the Equal Suffrage **Bill** gave the vote to women aged over 21, and marked an end to the struggle that had taken up so much of Emmeline's life. Her health was failing, and Christabel moved her into a London nursing home. Emmeline still refused to forgive or see Sylvia, but she did receive a warm letter from Adela in Australia. She died on 14 June 1928, just a month before her 70th birthday.

Ex-suffragettes stood guard around her coffin in St John's Church on London's Smith Square. On the day of the funeral, as the coffin was taken out to the hearse, both men and women fell to their knees, and many watching policemen were seen with tears in their eyes. More than 1000 women bearing Women's Social and Political Union flags accompanied the hearse to Brompton Cemetery, where Christabel and Sylvia stood awkwardly beside each other as their mother's coffin was lowered into the earth.

▶ *Emmeline Pankhurst's funeral.*

Legacy

The slow expansion of voting rights has been a key feature of European and North American history over the last two centuries. Sooner or later, it could well be argued, the women of Britain would have received the vote.

But history is made by people, and someone had to lead the struggle for **women's suffrage**, someone had to inspire other women to those feats of daring and bravery that marked the suffragette campaigns. That woman was Emmeline Pankhurst.

▲ *The statue of Emmeline Pankhurst near the Houses of Parliament.*

The courage of conviction

At the end of the 19th century, the idea of women receiving the vote was considered extremely **radical**. Emmeline Pankhurst and her fellow suffragettes had to triumph over enormous opposition, and the difficulties they faced should not be underestimated. They were faced not only by almost the whole weight of the male establishment, but also by a way of thinking which held that women were almost a separate species, and certainly not capable of taking on the same responsibilities as men. The suffragettes had to step beyond these attitudes, to risk being insulted for being unfeminine. And because there were no **democratic** options open to them, they also had to step beyond the law.

With the Pankhursts at their head, many women proved themselves willing to do so. Christabel's imaginative tactics were one reason for their success, Emmeline's persuasive powers and inspirational example were another. Emmeline was a brilliant speaker, capable of moving even the stoniest heart, yet she herself always stressed that the suffragettes' motto was 'Deeds Not Words'. She never asked any of her followers to do something that she was not prepared to do herself. She went to prison with them, she would even – if the government had been prepared to risk her death – have suffered the pain and indignity of **force-feeding** with them.

An unforgiving nature

Both she and Christabel were **dictatorial** by temperament. Their decision in 1906 not to allow a democratization of the Women's Social and Political Union (WSPU) drove out some of their most capable colleagues, and their refusal even to reconsider the more violent programme adopted in 1912 cost them the friendship of the Pethick-Lawrences, who had been more like family than political partners. Emmeline never spoke to them again, nor to her daughter Sylvia, after Sylvia had challenged the right of Emmeline and Christabel to decide WSPU policy on their own.

The single-mindedness of Emmeline and Christabel, their utter inability to accept that sometimes they might be wrong, was wonderfully effective when it came to winning a political war with the government, but it came at a terrible human cost. Throughout her adult life Emmeline fell out with those, like her father, Keir Hardie and the Pethick-Lawrences, who had been her greatest allies, and for the last fifteen years of her life she was **estranged** from two of her three daughters.

A fighter

Emmeline's husband Richard believed that ordinary people, given the chance, would make the world a better place, and his daughter Sylvia inherited that belief. But Emmeline (and Christabel) had a less optimistic view of humanity.

▼ *Emmeline Pankhurst, out in front as usual.*

She believed that ordinary people needed the direction and leadership of **middle-class** reformers like herself, and she set out to provide such direction and leadership. Her refusal to listen to other women may have prevented the suffrage movement from developing a wider and deeper challenge to existing social values, but it also prevented the movement from losing its focus and its unity in internal arguments. Emmeline Pankhurst was, above all else, a fighter. Once the battle had been joined, winning was all that interested her. When the battle was finally won, it was a victory for all women, not just for her.

Single-mindedness: the reward

'There are literal minds which suppose that Mrs Pankhurst faced obloquy [abuse] and prison to win votes for women. She did a greater thing than that. She suffered to remove from the mind of every young girl the sense that she is bound to a predestined inferiority. The strength of this woman was in her torrential emotions. For me it was Mrs Pankhurst's voice that revealed her. She spoke very quietly and simply, but her voice could give to the plainest statements an almost intolerable power to move. Others did the thinking and piled up the armoury of arguments. She alone had the genius to act as if nothing else in this wide world mattered.'

(English politician H. N. Brailsford, writing in the *Daily Herald* after Emmeline Pankhurst's death)

Timeline

1858	Emmeline Goulden born 14 July in Manchester.
1867	Second Reform Act extends male suffrage. Manchester **Women's Suffrage** Society founded.
1869	American Women's Suffrage Assoociation founded.
1872	Emmeline is sent to Ecole Normale in Paris.
1878	Meets Richard Pankhurst at rally in Manchester.
1879	Marries Richard Pankhurst.
1880	Birth of first daughter Christabel.
1882	Birth of second daughter Sylvia.
1884	Birth of first son Frank.
1885	Richard Pankhurst fights general election in Rotherhithe, London. Birth of third daughter Adela.
1886	Family moves to Hampstead Road, London. Sets up Emerson and Company shop.
1888	Death of first son Frank.
1889	Family moves to Russell Square, London. Birth of second son Harry. Founding of Women's Franchise League.
1893	Family returns to Manchester. New Zealand becomes the first country to give women the vote.
1894	Emmeline Pankhurst voted onto Board of **Poor Law** Guardians.
1896	Defies ban on public speaking at Boggart Hole Clough.
1898	Richard Pankhurst dies. Emmeline Pankhurst takes paying job as **Registrar of Births and Deaths**. Resigns from Board of Poor Law Guardians.
1903	Founding of Women's Political and Social Union (WSPU).
1905	Failure of latest **private member's** women's suffrage **bill**.
1906	*Daily Mail* invents term 'suffragettes'. First suffragettes go to Holloway Prison. Finland becomes the first European country to give women the vote.
1907	Several women leave WSPU over Pankhursts' **dictatorial** ways.

1908	Emmeline Pankhurst serves first prison sentence for leading assault on House of Commons.
	(June) Addresses Hyde Park rally attended by half a million.
1909	First suffragette **hunger strikes**.
	Emmeline Pankhurst leads battle in Parliament Square.
1910	Death of second son Harry.
	(Oct) 'Black Friday' battle in Parliament Square.
1912	Emmeline Pankhurst opens new 'militant' campaign by breaking **Downing Street** windows.
	Christabel escapes to Paris; campaign of **arson** begins.
	Pethick-Lawrences and others leave the WSPU over issue of violence.
1913	Bombing of several large houses.
	Emily Wilding Davison killed at the **Derby**.
1914	'Militant' campaign reaches a climax.
	Emmeline Pankhurst suspends suffragette campaign when World War I breaks out. Demands **industrial conscription** of women.
1916	Tours USA and Canada.
1917	Visits Russia.
1918	Tours USA and Canada. Women aged over 30 given the vote.
1919	Tours USA and Canada, and sets up home in latter.
1920	Becomes star speaker for Canadian health organization.
1924	Rests in Bermuda after health collapses.
1925	Opens teashop in South of France, then returns to England.
1926	Offers help to government during **General Strike.**
1927	Agrees to stand as **Conservative** at next election.
1928	Women aged over 21 given right to vote.
	Emmeline Pankhurst dies 14 June, aged 69 years.

Places to visit and further reading

Places to visit
Brompton Cemetery, Finborough Road, London SW10:
   location of Emmeline Pankhurst's grave
Pankhurst Centre, 60–62 Nelson Street, Manchester, Greater
   Manchester M13 9WP

Websites
Biography on the Time.com website by the British author
   Marina Warner:
www.time.com/time/time100/heroes/profile/pankhurst03.html
Biography link from the National Grid for Learning website:
www.spartacus.schoolnet.co.uk/ WpankhurstE.htm

Further reading
Emmeline Pankhurst, Linda Hoy, Hamilton, 1985
The Twentieth Century World (Living Through History series),
   Nigel Kelly, Rosemary Rees and Jane Shuter, Heinemann
   Library, 1998

Sources
My Own Story, Emmeline Pankhurst, Virago, 1979
The Pankhursts, David Mitchell, Heron, 1970
The Suffragette Movement, E. Sylvia Pankhurst, Virago, 1977

Key people of the time

Herbert Asquith (1852–1928) was **Liberal Party** leader and Prime Minister (1906–16) during the years of the suffragette campaign. A personal opponent of **women's suffrage**, he was a frequent target of suffragette actions. During his time in office he was also concerned with several other serious issues, most notably Irish Home Rule, the limiting of the powers of the House of Lords, and the outbreak of World War I.

Teresa Billington (later Greig) (1877–1964) joined the Women's Social and Political Union (WSPU) in December 1903 and became its second full-time organizer in the spring of 1905. She worked with Annie Kenney to build up the national headquarters in London, but then left the WSPU over the issue of democratization, and helped to form the Women's Freedom League.

Winston Churchill (1874–1965) was a prominent leader of the Liberal Government between 1906 and 1914, during the years of the suffragette campaign. He later joined the **Conservative** Party, and during the 1930s spoke out against the timid policy of successive British governments. He was an inspirational prime minister during the crucial early phase of World War II.

Emily Wilding Davison (1872–1913) was a schoolteacher and governess before joining the WSPU in November 1906. She was an organizer, frequent demonstrator, and one of the first women to go on **hunger strike** during one of her many prison sentences. She initiated the campaign of setting fire to postboxes in 1911, and was killed trying to stop the King's horse during the running of the Epsom **Derby** in 1913.

Keir Hardie (1856–1915) worked in the mines from the age of seven, eventually became a journalist, and was the first **socialist** to be elected a British Member of **Parliament** in 1892. The following year he became chairman of the newly founded **Independent Labour Party** (which over the next decade became one of the most important elements in the formation of the Labour Party). He was a friend of the Pankhursts (particularly Sylvia) and a strong believer in women's suffrage. He believed that war and violence are morally wrong and he opposed World War I.

Annie Kenney (1879–1953) met Christabel Pankhurst in 1905, and was her partner in the famous Free Trade Hall protest in October of that year. The following year she was sent to organize the WSPU in London with Teresa Billington. She was a frequent demonstrator and one of the WSPU's most popular speakers. In 1907–11 she was the party's organizer in the West of England; from 1912 to 1914 she acted as Christabel's representative in London, travelling to Paris each weekend to receive instructions for the following week's campaigning. After 1914 she supported Emmeline and Christabel's pro-war stance.

David Lloyd George (1863–1945) served as Asquith's **Chancellor of the Exchequer** (1905–15) during the years of the suffragette campaign. Midway through World War I he became prime minister.

Richard Pankhurst (1838–98) was a Manchester lawyer active in politics. He was an early socialist who believed in state ownership of land, workers' control in industry, universal free education, and the abolition of the monarchy and House of Lords. He was a campaigner for women's suffrage before he met and married Emmeline Goulden in 1878. He died in 1898.

Emmeline Pethick-Lawrence (1867–1954) became the WSPU's treasurer in 1906, and brought order to the organization's finances, becoming, in her own words, 'the solid foundation for the Pankhursts' genius'. She fell out with the Pankhursts in 1912 over their insistence in mounting a more violent campaign, but continued to work for women's suffrage.

Richard Pethick-Lawrence (1871–1961) provided the WSPU with financial help and organizational skill. He was the main architect of the famous Hyde Park rally in June 1908, and invented the term 'Cat and Mouse Act' for the government's policy of releasing hunger strikers until they had regained their strength, and then re-arresting them. Like his wife (see above) he fell out with the Pankhursts in 1912.

Glossary

amendment in Parliament, an addition to a bill

arson the deliberate burning of property

bill in Parliament, a draft version of a new law that is presented for discussion

Chancellor of the Exchequer British government minister responsible for running the economy

communism originally an extreme form of socialism, in which property is held communally (in common) rather than individually. The term 'communism' subsequently became associated with the dictatorial state and system of economic planning which was created in the Soviet Union during the 1920s and 30s.

Conservative Party one of two main British political parties since the 18th century, known as the Tory Party until the late 19th century

democratic reflecting the wishes of all those involved

dictator person who rules unrestricted by others

diphtheria acute bacterial illness

Downing Street street in central London; the prime minister's official residence is at number 10

dowry money or property that a bride gives to her new husband

estranged having once had a relationship, but refusing to continue to do so

executive committee decision-making group

fascism dictatorial system of government originating in Italy, which was later known for its aggressive nationalism. Nazism was one type of fascism.

force-feed force food into people who refuse to eat

General Strike simultaneous strike action in all industries in Britain in 1926

Home Secretary British government minister responsible for maintaining law and order

hunger strike refusing to accept food, as a political protest

Independent Labour Party (ILP) socialist political party formed in 1892, which was absorbed into the Labour Party around the turn of the century

industrial conscription forcing people to work in industry

Liberal Party one of two main British political parties in the late 19th and early 20th centuries

middle class the people in society who are educated to work as doctors, lawyers, teachers and in similar jobs, and do not usually need to do manual labour for a living

Paris Commune revolutionary government which seized power in Paris at the end of the Franco-Prussian War in 1871. It was overthrown by the French Army after ten weeks.

Parliament in the UK, the law-making body, comprising the House of Commons (containing Members of Parliament who are voted in by the public), House of Lords and monarch

patriotism love of one's country

Poor Law law that regulated government help to the poor. No one would be allowed to receive help unless they entered a workhouse and did a specified amount of work.

private member's bill bill introduced by an individual Member of Parliament

radical noun: someone who favours fundamental changes in society; adjective: far-reaching

Registrar of Births and Deaths official who keeps a record of births and deaths

Second Boer War war fought between Great Britain and the two Boer republics of Transvaal and the Orange Free State (1899–1902). The Boers wished to safeguard their independence; the British wanted to secure political rights for all citizens in the Boer Republics and to gain control of the southern African goldmines.

socialism a set of political ideas which puts more stress on the needs of the community as a whole and less on the needs of the individual

women's suffrage women's right to vote

Index

Titles in the *Leading Lives* series include:

Hardback   0 431 13865 6

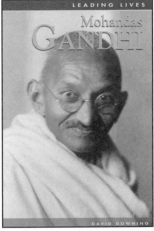

Hardback   0 431 13868 0

Hardback   0 431 13867 2

Hardback   0 431 13864 8

Hardback   0 431 13869 9

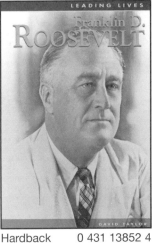

Hardback   0 431 13852 4

Find out about the other titles in this series on our website www.heinemann.co.uk/library